We Journey in Hope

We Journey in Hope

Reflections on the words from the Cross

Neil Paynter & Peter Millar

WILD GOOSE PUBLICATIONS

Contents of the book © the individual contributors
Compilation © 2011 Neil Paynter and Peter Millar

First published 2011 by
Wild Goose Publications
4th Floor, Savoy House, 140 Sauchiehall Street, Glasgow G2 3DH, UK
www.ionabooks.com
Wild Goose Publications is the publishing division of the Iona Community.
Scottish Charity No. SC003794. Limited Company Reg. No. SC096243.

ISBN 978 1 84952 076 8

Cover design © Wild Goose Publications from an idea by David Coleman

The publishers gratefully acknowledge the support of the Drummond Trust,
3 Pitt Terrace, Stirling FK8 2EY in producing this book.

A catalogue record for this book is available from the British Library.

Overseas distribution:
Australia: Willow Connection Pty Ltd, Unit 4A, 3-9 Kenneth Road,
Manly Vale, NSW 2093
New Zealand: Pleroma, Higginson Street, Otane 4170, Central Hawkes Bay
Canada: Novalis/Bayard Publishing & Distribution, 10 Lower Spadina Ave.,
Suite 400, Toronto, Ontario M5V 2Z2

Printed by Bell & Bain, Thornliebank, Glasgow

Mixed Sources
Product group from well-managed
forests and other controlled sources
www.fsc.org Cert no. TT-COC-002769
© 1996 Forest Stewardship Council

Contents

Dedicated to Leith Fisher

Introduction

Introduction

This small book is an invitation to listen and gaze with those who stand at the foot of the cross of Jesus. And more, we are encouraged to seek signs of the continuing Passion of God in the world, not in abstract ideas but in our human bodies and souls, in our willingness to absorb evil, suffering, grief and shame willingly. And yet more, to enter into Jesus's dying and rising, to feel part of the Passion.

As I read this manuscript, a book, a film and two friends came to mind.

The Last of the Just is a remarkable novel by André Schwarz-Bart. According to Jewish tradition, thirty-six men, 'the Lamed-waf', are born to take the burden of the world's suffering upon themselves. The old Jewish tradition tells of a figure that keeps on appearing within history. The form of the figure is tragic and yet therein lies the mystery. The one who is pain-bearer is also the one through whom liberation, healing, hope and life are released. The book concludes with the story of a figure wandering among the Jews of Europe heading for Auschwitz in 1943.

Of Gods and Men is a French film which has received wide acclaim. It tells the true story of a small Cistercian monastery, Our Lady of Atlas, situated on the edge of an impoverished Algerian village. The monks live happily with their Muslim neighbours until they come under threat from members of an Islamist armed group determined to drive non-Muslims from the country. Should they decide to stay or should they go? Is going cowardice? Is staying arrogance? Is martyrdom their destiny? The climax of the film is a Last Supper scene in which we see the men's careworn faces as they absorb the mystery of their own deaths. They were kidnapped in March 1997 and later executed. In June of the same year their bodies were brought back to the monastery and buried. A letter written by the superior of that small community, Dom Christian de Chergé, left instructions that it was to be opened upon his death. This text continues to be a source of meditation.

A friend tells of time spent in Belfast and of listening to women, Catholic and Protestant, whose husbands, sons, neighbours and friends had been killed, wounded, imprisoned during the Troubles in Northern Ireland. 'So this is the cross that you carry?' she said to the women. It became clear that after all this time, through all this suffering, these women had never made the connection between their own pain-bearing and cross-bearing. And that remains the case for many of us. We simply do not make the connection.

And another friend, a priest living with MS, has helped me to recognise that for some the faith journey includes the experience of dereliction, of God-forsakenness, of being apparently without faith in order to grow in faith.

In this book we are helped to listen yet again to the words from the Cross, to recognise the watermark within human history of God's continuing Passion in the world and, within our own life stories, to make the connections and to feel part of the Passion.

Donald Eadie

A note on how the words from the Cross came together

The seven 'words from the Cross' are expressions traditionally attributed to Jesus, spoken during his crucifixion, gathered from the Gospels of Matthew, Mark, Luke and John. This 'seven words' tradition is an example of the devotional method of reading the Bible in which material from different accounts is combined into a single account.

The first word concerning forgiveness is found in Luke's Gospel. The second word addressed to the thief who hangs alongside him is also in Luke, as is the seventh word in which Jesus places his spirit into the hands of God.

The third word, *'He is your son: she is your mother'*, is from John's Gospel.

The fourth word, *'My God, my God, why did you abandon me?'*, is found in Mark and Matthew.

The fifth word, *'I am thirsty'*, is again from John's account of the Crucifixion.

The sixth word, *'It is finished'*, is also from John.

The 'seven words' are often part of the Good Friday liturgy in churches around the world.

'Forgive them, Father.
They don't know
what they are doing'

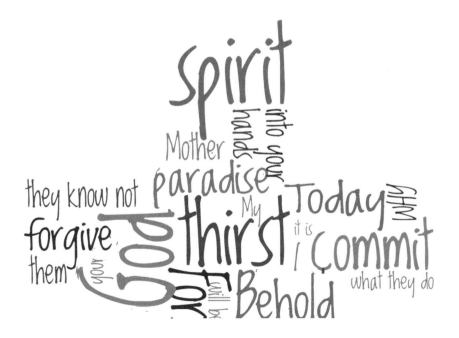

> *'Forgive them, Father! They don't know what they are doing.'*
> (Luke 23:34, GNB)

> *We come with self-inflicted pains*
> *of broken trust and chosen wrong,*
> *half-free, half-bound by inner chains,*
> *by social forces swept along,*
> *by powers and systems close confined*
> *yet seeking hope for humankind[1]*
> Brian Wren

A few years ago, with Anne McPherson, I wrote a book about a ministry we had shared, along with my late wife, Dorothy, in Bidwill in western Sydney. Bidwill carries many of the markers of modern social deprivation and is home to many cultures and religious traditions. In Bidwill, random violence and acts of sacrifice and love companion one another each day. In the foreword to the book, Jonathan Inkpin, an Australian friend, wrote some words about our world which are prophetic. In my understanding, Jonathan's words relate to these first words from the Cross:

> *The contemporary world provides a great paradox. The incredible diversity of the world's population is linked ever more closely by the forces of globalisation and the impact of climate change. Yet we remain deeply fractured by massive disparities of wealth and by conflicts intimately related to our varied cultures, religions and identities. Rather than divisions being transformed, past painful memories are regularly enlarged and new walls are daily erected. In the Western world, fear of 'the other' has been a powerful driver of recent social and political policy. Meanwhile, many people are now accustomed to knowing little or nothing of their next-door neighbours, still less of other postcodes.[2]*

At a time when new walls of division and fresh misunderstandings are becoming part and parcel of the fabric of humankind, the idea of forgiveness seems totally counter-cultural. Why should we forgive one another? Why should the nations forgive one another? How can we forgive past memories and earlier narratives within our communities or within our own often complicated lives? And why should the millions of our sisters and brothers who today remain trapped in gut-wrenching poverty and oppressive social structures even dream about forgiving the rest of us who, it can be argued, are directly and indirectly responsible for their marginalisation?

Throughout the centuries, theologians and biblical scholars have reminded us that these words of Jesus are in a sense a nutshell of the whole Gospel. They bring us to the mind and heart of God. Here in this situation of agony, Jesus, hanging on a rough cross, looked around at all who mocked him, and in tenderness invited God to forgive both their cruelty and their ignorance. Many of those gathered around the cross that day did not know what they were doing – in fact they had not the slightest clue as to what they were doing. They were blinded. Just as we are also constantly without sight or understanding in our own lives, or in Brian Wren's words, 'half-free, half-bound'. Like many of those at the foot of the cross, we too are swept along by forces which often desensitise us. How else can we explain the contemporary abuse of planet Earth and our corporate refusal to live more simply that others may survive?

As I was thinking about the many ways in which we easily remain ignorant about human need in our globalised, technological world, and our failures to find forgiving love in many situations within our own lives, I asked a friend, Sally Beaumont, who over the years has personally walked with many folk on the margins, how she responded to these first words from the Cross. This is Sally's reply:

Dear Peter,

Thank you for asking me to think about these words of Jesus.

From my perspective I feel there are three issues to which they could apply today.

Firstly, the government for which I vote, the government to which I happily pay taxes, the government who acts on my behalf, does not believe that nuclear weapons are immoral and obscene. For many years now I have protested at the Faslane base in the west of Scotland where the Trident submarines carrying nuclear weapons are kept on permanent alert. Should they ever be used, vast numbers of civilians would die and huge tracts of land be laid waste for generations to come. Why do those in power not realise this as millions of us do? Do they know what they are doing?

Secondly, I have been accommodating destitute asylum seekers now for several years. I am constantly appalled at some of the treatment meted out to them. The United Kingdom Border Agency does not seem to regard them as human beings but as objects. Trying to access information through the Home Office is nigh impossible, so a Member of Parliament told me. It is like a fortress. They and I are disrespected and harassed. Double standards are used, sometimes inadvertently, but nevertheless used. Do they not know how they are treating people?

Thirdly, for many years, I have been campaigning against sex-trafficking. It is a global trade now, near to overcoming the traffic in drugs. My comment is to all men. Without your selfish fixation with sex this could be eliminated. Do they not know what they are doing?

I hope these thoughts are helpful.

Sally, with love

In this note to me, Sally points clearly to areas in our common life where we need God's forgiveness and healing before we can rediscover our essential humanity. In his words, Jonathan Inkpin also reminds us of the places where our shared humanity is forgotten and severed. At the place called 'The Skull' there was not just one cross, but another two – one on either side of Jesus. The two men hanging on these other crosses are described as 'bandits' – a word which carries a certain ring even in our time. We know little of the details of their lives, but we can assume that somewhere along the line, these two guys went off the rails. However, whatever their failures may have been, at this pivotal moment in human history, they find themselves companions of Jesus.

And as he hung there between them, Jesus uttered words shot through with huge compassion. Words both for the men on either side of him, and for the crowd shouting all kinds of abuse at him. *'Forgive them, Father. They don't know what they are doing.'* He could have said other words, but it was these particular words which came from his lips. Forgiveness, freely offered. In the midst of his personal agony, Jesus was offering the possibility of inner liberation: of new hope, of a fresh way of looking at life. These were not words of condemnation, or of anger or of self-pity. Quite the opposite – as in themselves they revealed the tender-hearted mind of the One who holds and sustains the universe. Not a God of harsh judgement, but a God who understands how vulnerable we all are. Do you remember that little couplet which talks of the horse rider who had met with an accident and was about to die? The lines go as follows:

'Between the stirrup and the ground,
mercy I asked and mercy found.'

And while it is true that the idea of forgiveness may be counter-cultural in a secular society, what is also true is that the reality of being able to forgive is almost a prerequisite if even a few of our present global disconnections are to be lessened. To let go of bitterness, anger and hatred but also, in tandem with that letting go, to come to an ever clearer knowledge of our ignorance of so much that is going on within the human family. To walk with a certain degree of humility, and to be prepared to have our mind changed as we come to see situations in a different light. Perhaps even to begin to recognise that 'the image of God' is carried in us all, and that every human being is precious to the Creator.

An old hymn, familiar in many churches, stills ring true in a world of high technology:

> *Dear Lord and Father of us all,*
> *forgive our foolish ways;*
> *reclothe us in our rightful mind;*
> *in purer lives your service find,*
> *in deeper reverence, praise.*[3]

And these words also gently remind us that forgiving often begins at home, within our own four walls. A task, as we all know, often fraught with obstacles! To forgive the partner who has totally let you down; to forgive the child who has turned against you; to forgive the mum or dad who abandoned you; to forgive the one who abused you; to forgive that person who makes your life a living hell every day. I don't think we can forgive in any real way, without the help and presence of the One who understands us so much better than we understand ourselves. I certainly know that to be true in my own life. It's so easy to harbour resentments, silent angers and cruel judgements. And to harbour them long-term – even sometimes for a lifetime! If we are honest with ourselves there are times when we feel anything but forgiving or forgiven. A short, yet profound prayer used by the Iona Community has helped me to refocus both on God's forgiving love toward me and on my ability to forgive others.

> *May God forgive you,*
> *Christ renew you,*
> *and the Spirit enable you to grow in love …*[4]

In the light of these words which mirror those of Jesus, I have come to understand the first words from the Cross as an invitation from God to realise that we need not be imprisoned within these resentments and angers which use up our emotional energy. There is liberation for the individual soul, and at a global level. Wherever we see genuine acts of reconciliation among peoples, we see God's forgiving love at work. The late Fred Kaan understood this truth when he wrote: *'Let love suggest my mode, my mood of living.'*[5]

Prayer

> *From a place of agony*
> *as death drew near,*
> *you offered surprising words of life.*
> *Words of tenderness –*
> *elevating our human condition*
> *in their invitation to move beyond*
> *our imprisoning angers –*
> *to that place where*
> *all souls can sing of freedom*
> *in the light of your forgiveness.*

Peter Millar

Notes

1. Brian Wren, from the hymn 'Great God, your love has called us here', words © 1975, 1995 Stainer & Bell Ltd

2. Jonathan Inkpin, from Campfires and Wellsprings in Surprising Places, by Anne McPherson and Peter Millar, Wellspring Community (www.wellspringcommunity.org.au/links.php)

3. John Greenleaf Whittier (adapted)

4. From the Iona Community's 'Act of Prayer'

5. Fred Kaan, from 'Today I live, one day shall come my death' words © 1975 Stainer & Bell Ltd

'I promise you that today
you will be in Paradise with me'

> *One of the criminals hanging there hurled insults at him: 'Aren't you the*
> *Messiah? Save yourself and us!' The other one, however, rebuked him,*
> *saying, 'Don't you fear God? You received the same sentence he did. Ours,*
> *however, is only right, because we are getting what we deserve for what*
> *we did; but he has done no wrong.' And he said to Jesus, 'Remember me,*
> *Jesus, when you come as king!' Jesus said to him, 'I promise you that today*
> *you will be in Paradise with me.' (Luke 23:39–43, GNB)*

Even as we read these verses 2000 years after the event, we encounter something of the human intimacy between these three men brought together in
suffering. They were all near death, in excruciating pain. And in our own
time, when people are still being hung up to die in more than a few countries, it is not beyond our imagination to visualise something of this situation. The abusive crowd, the grieving family, the sorrow-filled devotees.
Above them hung these men in their final moments and in brief conversation. Each of them understanding their agony differently. It's a scene that for
me mirrors many of the violent, cruel deaths which daily, it seems, we see
on TV. Death in the raw. A long way from a gentle passing in a warm room
at the end of a comfortable life! Brian Wren captured the desolation of it all:

> *Here hangs a man discarded,*
> *a scarecrow hoisted high,*
> *a nonsense pointing nowhere*
> *to all who hurry by.*[1]

And yet, and yet, in the midst of this dereliction we have these words of
Jesus for the guy at his side! This tortured, abandoned soul asks Jesus if he
can travel with him into the heart of God's love and light – and Jesus says
'Yes.' Do we need to know more?

I never thought you would understand,
you were so different from me –
but my question stumbled out,
and You invited me home.[2]

And it's this knowledge – whatever language we employ – that many search for today. I mean by that, the realisation that when push comes to shove we are actually held in the arms of God. That, ultimately, all of our struggles, pains and laughter will be embraced in a framework of meaning. My friend John Bell of the Iona Community expresses this truth so powerfully in these lines: '*Take, O, take me as I am; summon out what I shall be; set your seal upon my heart and live in me.*'[3]

'Paradise' is originally a Persian word, meaning 'a walled garden'. The place where the king walked and entertained his closest friends. The place of honour and of friendship within the palace compound, where intimacies could be exchanged and celebrated. And for our Muslim friends, 'Paradise' is that garden of delights and Peace which the Koran promises the faithful after death. And these meanings of the word help me to come to a deeper understanding of what Jesus on that day was offering the fearful man beside him.

Even though I myself (along with most folk!) have little understanding of the life beyond this one, what I do believe from this encounter between these two dying men is that God always sees beyond our human frailties and constantly seeks to 'summon out' that person who we truly are. And in that summoning out, the image of God is set within our minds and hearts, both in life, and in death. Our souls are sealed for a journey which continues well beyond our few years on earth, but the nature of that journey remains a mystery and is matter of belief, of faith.

A further jewel in this whole drama – and given my own spiritual questioning over the years, a wonderful jewel – relates to the attitude of Jesus. In his response to the criminal's question, Jesus cuts through much of that unedifying legalism which is often a marker of institutional Christianity. He does not ask him if he is rich or poor, black or white, gay or straight, or divorced, or educated, or employed, or homeless – he does not even ask him the nature of his crime! Nothing of that. Jesus sees him as a fellow human being in need of God's love. And it was going to be this very day – before the sun goes down – that he would be with him in Paradise. No purgatory or interim stopping places are mentioned here! They came later on when analytical minds like my own preferred doctrinal certainties over the risk-filled chaos of limitless love.

Brother Roger, the founder of the ecumenical Taizé Community in France who was murdered while at prayer, touched the lives of thousands. Everything he wrote was embedded in his prayer life and that is why his words continue to help many of us in the world. He understood that God is continually reaching out to all peoples – that it truly is limitless love of the kind embodied in the words of Jesus to the criminal. And Brother Roger expressed it this way:

> *Can you perceive it? Can you discern it? When your night becomes dark, God's love is a fire. Perhaps the fire is under the ashes and no longer gives you light. Perhaps, overcome by doubt, you are asking yourself: 'But where is God? Has he gone silent?' The Spirit of God is always in you – never absent from your life. The resonance of God's voice is within you. He always offers us somewhere to rest our heart.*[4]

And this great promise of a place to rest our heart in the wider possibilities of God's love is a strong challenge to the present religious fundamentalisms which dominate much of modern thinking: the belief that the way I understand God is right and the way in which you understand God is wrong. The global fundamentalisms which plague our time are not leading to acceptance or love or understanding, but to wars and rumours of wars, and in many places to an unending cycle of violence. We weep at all of this – sorrowful that religion appears to be bringing misery to our human family which is actually connected by the same heartbeat.

These second words from the Cross are propelling us to reach out across these soul-destroying barriers – as Jesus did all through his ministry – and to discover in multiple ways a wider knowledge of the divine. A task which holds enormous challenges and asks of us profound spiritual insight. It is a task for all the great religious traditions of the world (as the great German theologian Hans Küng made clear many years ago in his writings) and for all those who hold no formal belief in a god but who love humanity. And it is, thankfully, a task already begun in millions of human hearts. It cannot be otherwise when we know that every day, in every place on earth, people of all faiths and of none are challenging the voices of violence, of oppression and of injustice through acts of self-sacrifice, of courage and of risk-taking compassion.

We are not abandoned. We journey in hope. Our hearts can still sing, even in dark days. And in the last moments of his life on earth, the man hanging beside Jesus in that place of apparently ultimate abandonment discovered these truths for himself. He returned home, rejoicing. And in the walled garden encountered the face of Love.

Prayer

Let me pause and be still for a moment
and remember that each day
the One who sustains all of life
offers me a place in which to rest my soul
so that I may grow in love.

Peter Millar

Notes

1. Brian Wren, from the song 'Here hangs a man discarded', words © 1975, 1995 Stainer & Bell Ltd

2. Peter Millar

3. John L. Bell, from the chant 'Take, O, take me as I am', Come All You People: Shorter Songs for Worship, John L. Bell and the Wild Goose Resource Group, Wild Goose Publications © Wild Goose Resource Group

4. Brother Roger, from a Letter from Taizé

'Woman, here is your son …
Here is your mother'

> *Near the cross of Jesus stood his mother, his mother's sister, Mary the wife of Clopas, and Mary Magdalene. When Jesus saw his mother there, and the disciple whom he loved standing nearby, he said to her, 'Woman, here is your son,' and to the disciple, 'Here is your mother.' From that time on, this disciple took her into his home. (John 19:25–27, NIV)*

Jesus came into the world in a messy confusion of family relationships, drenched in blood. He dies as he was born, changing the pattern of dominant family relationships, drenched in blood.

Just as at his birth, Joseph becomes his foster father; so at his death, John becomes Mary's foster son through God's own word and agency of care. For thousands of years people have been fascinated by the way Jesus's family is both out of the ordinary and yet very ordinary, creating a community of love beyond the ties of blood. This is a family which, as announced at the beginning of John's Gospel, is *'not of natural descent, nor of human decision or a husband's will, but born of God'* (NIV).

In this extraordinary, painful time of his dying Jesus does something which is quite ordinary. He takes a moment, between laboured breaths, to leave instructions for the care of his kindred and with those closest to him. He makes his 'will', as it were, using the legal formula of the Jewish people, language in which a first-born son traditionally makes provision for those for whom he had responsibility.

In the Law of Moses, care for the widow and the orphan, for the stranger and for the poor was a primary provision. The Bible offers plenty of stories where this care is offered: Ruth and Naomi, Moses in his basket, the persistent widow demanding justice from the unjust judge. Widows especially would often live in penury, and at the cross Mary is facing the scandal of material poverty. Given the oppressive upheaval surrounding Jesus's death, Mary may also have been facing exile once again. At this moment in the story Mary embodies and symbolises the most precarious of situations, and those from which the Law of the Hebrew scriptures offers protection. Jesus acts, practically, to make a new family relationship. It is an action of speech, God's creative word, which brings the world into being, reconfiguring family love, so that it is, to repeat, *'not of natural descent, nor of human decision or a husband's will, but born of God'*.

It is quite usual for people who know that they do not have long to live to look to ensure that they make their peace; deal with matters that could cause their families difficulties and additional suffering. Jesus, in this third word from the Cross, acts to do likewise by making arrangements for the care of his mother and his Beloved Disciple, John. In the Anglican Litany the following words of prayer acknowledge that at these times of life, time to prepare and to take care is to be desired:

... and from dying suddenly and unprepared,
Good Lord, deliver us.

Rowan Williams reflects on his experience in New York on September 11th, 2001 and on the 'Last Words' of that day – testimonies of those receiving telephone calls from the planes, calls to say goodbye and to offer final words of care and love.

Someone who is about to die in terrible anguish makes room in their mind for someone else; for the grief and terror of someone they love. They do what they can to take some atom of that pain away from the other by the inarticulate message on the mobile. That moment of 'making room' is what I as a religious person have to notice. It isn't 'pious', it isn't

> *language about God; it's simply language that brings into the world*
> *something other than self-defensiveness. It's a breathing space.*[1]

And so it is with Jesus, fully human in his dying; 'making room' in the simplest of words for his mother, and her new son, and keeping her, following Jewish Law and tradition, from penury and the loneliness of widowhood.

This is a powerful example of re-creation, of how Jesus's words reconfigure the natural order of family. John is not Mary's son; Mary is not John's mother – but under the will of God, through its traditional formulation in Jewish Law, families can be radically reconfigured. Such radical reconfigurations of family are part of the routine story of any oppressed people. Children are orphaned, fathers and brothers disappear, are found dead, women are left widowed, friends are held guilty by association. As people run and flee, grieve and mourn, new practical ways of caring emerge from the messy chaos and confusion which is part of the experience of persecution and oppression.

In a church I attend at times, the diaspora from one of the world's most oppressed countries – Eritrea – gather to sing praise and to hope.

> *Despite its small population of four million, the country's alarming*
> *record of human rights violations has caused it to be ranked as the*
> *second largest source of refugees in the world (in absolute numbers). By*
> *end of 2008, Eritrea produced 62,700 new asylum seekers around the*
> *world. The simplest arithmetic model translates this into 5225 refugees*
> *per month. In this regard, Eritrea was preceded only by Zimbabwe which*
> *had 118,500 new claims in 2008. Even failed or chaotic states, such as*
> *Somalia and Iraq, which have greater population numbers than Eritrea,*
> *were preceded by Eritrea in relation to new refugee outflow.*[2]

In Tigrinya-speaking congregations in exile we find unaccompanied minors, foster children, stepfathers, cousins, lone parents, mothers who do not know if the father of their child is dead or alive. We find these constellations are quite normal for these congregations, as they are today also, for example, in the Occupied Territories. And it would have been so in Roman Occupied Palestine.

This work of caring under the will of God, in reconfigurations of family, is often hampered by UK Border Agency regulations. Nonetheless, this story registers in the official statistics, where such turmoils of war at home are a fading memory. The UK Office of National Statistics' Survey of Social Trends and Household Composition reports around 150,000 widowhoods each year. It estimates that *'there are over 87,000 children and young people looked after on any given day in the UK. Of these children, around 73,000 are looked after away from home, almost four-fifths of whom (over 57,000 or around 78 per cent) live with at least 45,000 foster families'.*[3]

That families are torn apart by grief, war, poverty and oppression is something we know all too well. Jesus's words to his mother and his Beloved Disciple create a new community of kinship – not part of the natural order, but ordered under the will of God. Jesus's act of making space as he dies continues what he did throughout his life. He makes room for the systems of death and domination to be countered by newness, by love, by justice and by hope. These simple words of a son to a mother and to a new son are a counter-script to the words which would destroy human care and loveliness. Jesus dies as he lived, with words which very simply and intimately act against the grain of fear and domination.

Jesus condemned all forms of domination:

Patriarchy and the oppression of women and children
The economic exploitation and the impoverishment of the entire classes
of people
The family as chief instrument for the socialisation of children into
oppressive roles and values
Hierarchical power arrangements that disadvantage the weak while
benefiting the strong
The subversion of the law by defenders of privilege (cf. persistent widow)
Rules of purity that keep people separated
Racial superiority and ethnocentrism
The entire sacrificial system with its belief in sacral violence.[4]

In one simple loving speech-act, Jesus overturns each of these forms of oppression. Even under torture and death he is seen struggling in solidarity against the scandal that is poverty and in accordance with the most radical of Jewish laws.[5] This, too, is a moment of incarnation, for to incarnate God is to be fully human. John and Mary respond with love and hospitality, poor enough in spirit to be open at this point of deepest grief to God's will, and to understand what it means to be children of God. Mary already knew, from the beginning, how to say 'Yes' to God, letting her life willingly be transformed under the orderings of God's will so that God's Son could indeed be incarnate. Now, at the cross, Mary and John are commissioned in a most intimate way to love one another in place of one who has gone, so that a new community may be formed, liberated from endless grief and from poverty.

'Woman, here is your son ...
Here is your mother.'

A small litany for mothers and sons

From the scandal of poverty and persecution
from narrow understandings
from families that say they are complete
Good Lord, deliver us.

From believing my children must be of my body
from believing mothers must be made of my blood
from being determined by our genes
Good Lord, deliver us.

From pious words and sanctimony
from presuming to know anything of dying
from having no one to wait with us or for us
Good Lord, deliver us.

From all forms of violence
from systems of domination
from our part in both,
and from dying unprepared
Good Lord, deliver us.

Alison Swinfen

Notes

1. *Rowan Williams,* Writing in the Dust, *pp.4-5, Hodder and Stoughton, 2002*

2. *Daniel R. Mekonnen,* Importing a Transitional Justice Agenda into the Eritrean Human Rights Debate, *2011*

3. *Office of National Statistics: www.statistics.gov.uk/downloads/theme_social/Social-Trends40/ST40_Ch02.pdf*

4. *Walter Wink,* The Human Being: Jesus and the Enigma of the Son of Man, *p.14, Fortress Press, 2002.*

5. *Gustavo Gutiérrez,* A Theology of Liberation: History, Politics and Salvation, *p.267, SCM Press, 2001*

'My God, my God,
why have you forsaken me?'

'My God, my God, why have you forsaken me?' (Mark 15:34, NRSV)

Meditating on the Crucifixion is like standing on a storm-swept headland, watching as a ship is wrecked on the shore. There are few redeeming features of a shipwreck when rescue is impossible, and the same is true of the Crucifixion.

Instinctively we clutch at anything that can give us comfort. The loving words – *'Father, forgive them …'*; the assurance that the thief will be with Jesus in Paradise; the gentleness with which Jesus commits his mother into the care of the Beloved Disciple and him into hers; the words of committal – *'Father, into your hands I commend my spirit.'* Even the words *'I thirst'* and *'It is finished'* have a certain dignity about them.

Crucifixion is brutal in the extreme but at least these things may give us a few crumbs of comfort.

But then, out of the raging seas of destruction, there rears up a dark and terrible rock that seems to tear the heart out of the ship. It inflicts a mortal injury just when it seemed there could be no greater pain than to see someone we love put to death.

Mark says Jesus cried out in a loud voice: *'My God, my God, why have you forsaken me?'* No other words. There is just one more great cry in the darkness and then death.

We turn hopefully to Matthew, who sometimes has a gentler touch than the abrasive Mark – but there is no comfort here either.

Then, from somewhere long ago, we hear another voice. The voice of an old man holding a child in his arms. He gives thanks to God: *'Lord, now let your servant depart in peace. For my eyes have seen your salvation.'*

But then comes Simeon's dark warning to Mary: *'A sword shall pierce your heart also'* (Luke 2:29–30).

Perhaps it is as Jesus utters that terrible cry of abandonment that Mary's heart is truly pierced by the sword. The moment not only when her beloved child is dying but when he seems to be catastrophically abandoned by God; the one even closer to him than she has been.

To feel abandoned by God is a terrible experience. Many of us have had it at some time or another. The empty darkness is overwhelming. But for Jesus who always walked so closely with God, been part of God, it must have been immeasurably worse.

And yet. And yet, that is not the worst. Worse by far is that small word 'why'.

'My God, my God, WHY have you forsaken me?'

When we feel abandoned by God we know, or we may suspect, that it is in fact we who have closed our hearts and minds to His love. We are sinful, often stupid; we make mistakes and get things wrong. Very wrong. Wrong with our neighbour. Wrong with God. We know the story of the Prodigal Son (sometimes it may be we know it too well). We know deep in our hearts that God has not abandoned us – it's just that through the grime-covered lenses of our eyes we cannot see or feel God's presence.

Is that how it was with Jesus? Whatever else, he always seems to have had a clear vision of God. Such a close and intimate love of the Father that they almost seem as one. *'To know me is to know the Father,'* Jesus said. So how can he be abandoned by God? How can he ask the question 'why' have you abandoned me?

Unless, at the end, he suddenly loses his faith. That it bursts like a balloon and there is nothing there. And the whole Incarnation miracle ends with a whimper. Who knows?

Well, it may be there is an answer to that. Perhaps someone does know. And it may be he is the most inappropriate person on the face of the planet. The man most likely to hold Jesus in utter contempt.

Someone who knows well how to recognise courage and cowardice in other people. Someone who knows death and has inflicted it often and without hesitation. A hard man. Perhaps a cruel man. A man who is there at the Crucifixion and is watching closely – because that is his job.

Who is he? He is the executioner.

The actual words vary from Gospel to Gospel but, essentially, the Roman officer in charge of the execution says: *truly this was a great man; a heroic man; a son of God.* He might even have said: *truly this was the Son of God.*

What drew from this hard man such respect that he spoke his thoughts out loud, even when such words might have led to disciplinary action? It is not likely to have been a pathetic whimper from a crushed spirit. More likely he saw in the dying moments of Jesus a faith and a courage that he recognised as heroic.

So how can we reconcile the despair and hopelessness of abandonment by the Father with such dignity and courage?

It is unlikely the Roman officer was familiar with Psalm 22. In fact it's possible he did not even speak the language of Jesus. But Jesus must have been familiar with the psalm – all of it. The apparent despair of its opening verses – and the courageous faith of its later verses.

There is no way we can theorise about what those terrible words of abandonment meant to Jesus as he hung dying on the cross. Except that he chose them. He did not say: 'Father, where are you?' Or 'Father, why have you gone away?' Or 'Father, come back to me.' Or 'Father, please help me.' He spoke the opening words of Psalm 22.

We are not forensic scientists and this is not a religious version of *Silent Witness*. But wondering about his actual words and why he spoke them, and if he spoke them, is important. Apart from anything else, it leads us to confront another painful question. A question that involves us today.

The question is simply: where were the men? There's a lot in the gospels about the Twelve and about Peter being the first among them. Sometimes it is as though there were no women disciples: no courageous, faithful, loving, committed women around. It is as though they have been airbrushed out of the picture.

But when it came to the crunch (and this was definitely the crunch) where were these male leaders? Were they standing there exposed to danger with the small group of women, and possibly the Beloved Disciple? Apparently not. Jesus might have been forgiven if he had cried from the cross: 'My God, my God, why have they abandoned me?'

And how often in *our* lives do we abandon Jesus? ... Why, in the world of the 21st century, do we so often fail you? Why, despite your infinite and unconditional love, do we deny you? Why, when we see the suffering of our neighbours across the globe, and of this beautiful planet which is your wonderful creation, do we walk past on the other side?

Every day of our lives we turn away, run away. We busy ourselves with lesser things. Often churchy things. Every day we abandon God in our neighbour. How can we sleep in our beds while 25,000 of God's children starve to death every day? While people in our own cities die silently of poverty, cold and neglect?

Perhaps Jesus is still crucified today in situations of our own making. 'My God, my God, why do these people who are my disciples abandon me?'

What if? What if when old Simeon took the Christ child in his arms and spoke that terrible warning to Mary … what if he wasn't just speaking to her. What if he was looking past her, looking over her shoulder, into the future? What if he was also speaking to us?

Telling us that if we love this Christ child and follow this Christ person, the sword will enter our hearts too. At the sight of one we love put to death by the fear and greed of the world. But also at the realisation that it is not the Father but we ourselves who abandon him.

Prayer

Loving Father, this isn't a prayer so much as a car crash. They always happen as if in slow motion. First there's the terrible sound of the impact, the breaking of glass and pieces of metal flying everywhere. And then, for a moment, there is silence.

The impact is when he says those words: 'My God, my God. Why have you forsaken me?' And the world seems to fall apart and there's wreckage everywhere.

It tears at our hearts to see someone we love in pain. But what hurts even more is the knowledge that it's not you but we who have forsaken him. When we see him in our neighbour, hungry and naked, and we walk past on the other side.

And the realisation of our failure feels like the end of everything. And there is silence. But it's not the end. Because in the silence we hear the sound of someone running. Running towards us. A Father running to embrace a beloved child. Thank you.

Amen

David Rhodes

‘I thirst’

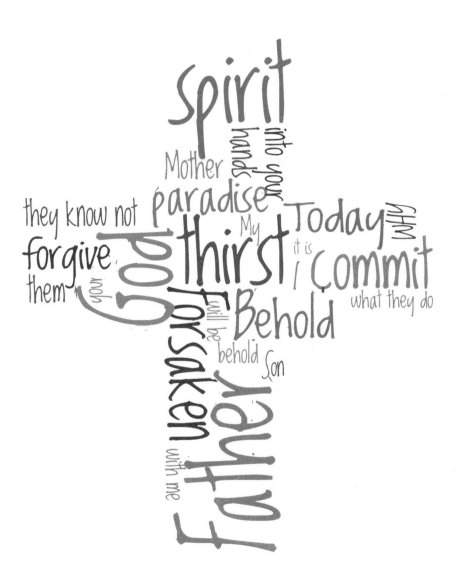

'*I thirst*' *(John 19:28 KJB/AV)*

I thirst

The heat of the midday sun beats back
from the bare rocks of this hilltop,
from the bleached wood of this cross.
The last time this man saw water
was when Pilate washed the blood-guilt from his hands.
The last time it passed these cracked lips
was at table with his friends –
who have now run away like raindrops into the thirsty earth.

I thirst

He imagines water flowing down a river-bed
after the spring rains, when the land is green,
where trees grow at the water's edge,
and – watched by kingfishers in their branches
and by crowds from the city along the bank –
two men wade into the Jordan,
waist deep in the still unpolluted waters.
John cupped his hand and raised it,
a rosary of bright drops falling as he poured water
over this head that is now beaded with blood.
Then the dove came down out of a clear heaven
and a voice proclaimed, 'This is my beloved son …'
But now the only words under the empty sky are

I thirst

'Son,' said his mother at the wedding,
'there is no wine left!'
And he laughed, 'What's that to me?'
But now, when his hour has come, he remembers
that in the courtyard there stood six stone water jars –
huge and full to the brim with cool pure water –
and that he sent the servants
to draw all the wine that they wanted –
to quench everyone's thirst,
enliven the party and celebrate human love.
That was a sign, water into wine,
just as much as the voice from heaven.
Folk said then that the host had left the best till last.
But at last, for the man on the cross, water will do:

I thirst

'Give me a drink,' he had said
to the woman at the well outside the city;
her look mingled wonder and mockery:
'You, a Jewish man, ask for a drink from a Samaritan woman?'
So many prejudices, prohibitions, dangers of misunderstanding.
Water was the one simple thing.
He remembers how thirsty he was,
sitting there by the well.
She drew water out of its depths,

the bucket overflowing, splashing, echoing,
precious water coming up dark and then flashing gold
as she poured it out in the sunshine.
The traveller drank his fill,
letting it caress his throat, grinning in gratitude,
splashing it on his face, his hands, his dusty feet,
making free with the water that was her gift.
Then the talk turned to living water –
a gift to her she didn't, at first, understand.
But she had understood his human need:

I thirst

His friends hadn't understood,
when he took the basin and the towel,
and washed their feet.
The upper room was filled with baffled silence,
the slip-slop of water, words of protest,
uncertain laughter. But his gentle hands
turned a routine task into a sign of caring:
the water blessed them, brought them together.
Though they drank wine that night,
for some the water was what they remembered:
the washing, the water poured out for them.
And it went on flowing through their lives.
As his life ebbs, he calls out again

I thirst

The soldiers raise a sponge soaked in sour wine, vinegar,
to his parched lips. It is as sharp
as the barbed wire and the minefields along the Jordan;
as cheap as booze which people drink to forget
and as stale as a marriage that doesn't work out;
as bitter as the divisions between men and women,
rich and poor, races, different faiths;
it silences the cry for justice
and it leaves a bad taste in the mouth;
it is as numbing as our guilt, as our fear of being loved.

This man's life was living water. Is this the last word?

I thirst

Jan Sutch Pickard

*Drawing on John 19:28–30; John 1:31–33; John 2:1–11; John 4:4–15; John
13:3–15*

‘It is finished’

'It is finished.' (John 19:30, NRSV)

The door closed for the last time. Our church building, opened with high hopes in a new housing scheme in the 1950s, became a thriving congregation full of love and energy and compassion. But for too long, it had been a sorry sight; frankly, an embarrassment. If you'd passed it, you would have had no inkling that there was any life there. Then, last summer, we had to switch off the gas because of a leak and the decision was made not to spend any money on fixing it. When it became too cold, we moved out to a local hall, wondering if we'd ever move back. Then, with winter's freezing temperatures, pipes burst, ceilings dripped, wooden floors buckled, carpets squelched and, at the coldest times, icicles clung to radiators. We turned the electricity off. The building is now unsafe, no longer fit to be home. It is finished. Or … It is finished!

Funny the difference an exclamation mark makes. *Take a moment to think about the difference it brings to this story of our church …*

For me, the full stop expresses a sense of:

- loss – 'we've lost something precious that's been an important part of our lives for a long time'

- inevitability – 'it had to come' 'prolonging the decision really wasn't helping'

- despair – 'how will we cope?' 'what will we do now?' 'it will never be the same again' 'this will be the end of the congregation, you'll see'

The exclamation mark, on the other hand, suggests a sense of:

- a more positive relief – 'thank goodness it's over!' 'much as we have loved the building, it just wasn't the right place for us any longer'

- a task completed – 'that building has seen a lot of life!' 'it's a place where Christian faith has been proclaimed and lived'

- permission to let go – 'we've had good and sad times there but now we can move on …'

- hope for the future – 'it's almost like starting again' 'what a sense of freedom and release'

That change of a single punctuation mark is all the difference between giving you, the reader, the sense that the life of the congregation is over, and suggesting that we are keeping on – and, of course, we are, with confident hope! The doors of that church building may be closed but the doors of the church – our hearts, minds and spirits – are assuredly not!

The Body of Christ – saddened, grieving, full of memories of our old building – lives on. We are letting go of our past bricks and mortar but we've not given up. Part of our story has ended; a chapter has closed and, as Mr Magorium said to Molly in the film *Mr Magorium's Wonder Emporium* as he prepared to die: *'I'm only asking you to turn the page, continue reading … and let the next story begin.'* It's early days but that's what we're doing; the next chapter, the next story – and our role in it – may be very different. But no way are we thinking of a full stop!

As I turned my quotes calendar over to December, month of Advent anticipation, there were words of the American author Louis L'Amour: *'There will come a time when you believe everything is finished. That will be the beginning.'* And as I nodded in agreement, I thought: Isn't that what resurrection is – both a continuation and a new beginning, inspired, encouraged, made possible by the infusion of the Holy Spirit?

> *'Now the green blade rises from the buried grain;*
> *wheat that in the dark earth many days has lain.'*

Returning to punctuation and to Jesus's words from the Cross 'It is finished': I checked twenty-two versions of the Bible, from the 400-year-old King James Version to contemporary versions like *The Message*. Twelve went for a full stop at the end and ten for an exclamation mark. *How does that change the way we hear Jesus uttering those words?*

His death was very close – and considering the pain and other physical consequences of crucifixion, I imagine Jesus would have been desperate for release, for it all to finish. Was that what he meant? 'My life is over.' I can't believe there isn't some truth in that.

But can't there be another, deeper meaning? That that which is finished resonates with a sense of accomplishment, fulfilment? Of the twenty-two Bible versions I looked up, only two used 'accomplished' and one used 'fulfilled' (the rest translated the Greek as 'finished' or 'done'). I find these two words hold a truth we may know intuitively but that we need to hear and speak aloud ourselves. Jesus knew his life was not only a gift from God – *'You are my Son, whom I love. I am pleased with you!'* – but a gift to be developed and shared for the sake of bringing closer God's Reign of Unconditional Love. That, after all, is God's mission. 'It is finished!' is surely a cry that he has accomplished his part in that mission. A part which, for me, is unique and remarkable given its long-lasting and worldwide effect.

But, it doesn't end there. There is no full stop. Whatever we may understand by resurrection (which for me is a living mystery) Jesus's life and Jesus's words from the Cross are sacraments of freedom and hope. Sacraments that it is now our risk and joy and purpose to live out in our lives – not simply as truths to be believed but as truths to be incarnated again and again, infused and embraced by the same Holy Spirit that infused and embraced the Man from Nazareth. *How far are we willing to allow that infusion and embrace to draw us ever deeper into God's Reign of Love?*

And it doesn't end with me! There is no full stop there either for *'No-one is an island, entire of itself'.* This unfinished task of incarnation is not for any one person alone – even Jesus. He knew that, as he gathered around him men and women to play their various and varied parts in God's mission. And so, with us – whichever limb of the Body of Christ we are. *How are we intentionally joining with other daughters and sons of God in whom God is well pleased (yes, even you!), in worship and mission, in the continuing incarnation of Love on earth? Please try to reflect on a positive answer rather than jump into the downward spiral of guilt.*

But there is no full stop even with the intentional community of Jesus's followers! Just as he taught and healed and affirmed the *anawim* – the lost and forsaken, the unwashed and unloved – the continuing task is not about 'us' doing it 'for them' – we're all in it together – regardless of our differences in culture, ethnicity, wealth and social status, religion, sexual orientation, gender, ability or anything else. God's Reign of Love is for us all to enjoy and be challenged by and take risks for. So may we all be able to believe of ourselves and each other, when our earthly life is ending, 'It is finished!'

Prayer

What did you mean, Jesus,
when you said 'It is finished'?
What had finished?
Your short life on earth
and even shorter ministry?
Why did you let it all end
when you'd barely begun?
You were doing so well.
Why did you have to go to Jerusalem
when you knew,
you knew what was likely to happen?
You could have stayed in Galilee
in the hills
away from danger.
The people would still have found you
and been taught
and healed
and affirmed.
Why, WHY?
OK, OK, I know the answer.
It's just hard
not so much to understand what you did and why
but to take on board what I must now do
to follow in your footsteps
and continue what you began.

O God,
help me.
It feels like you're expecting so much
yet it's true
even in my small experience
that as I discover my role in your mission
to incarnate your Reign of Love
I discover other friends of Jesus doing the same
(and not all of them in church).
And as I take a tiny risk to do or say something that points to truth
yet makes me feel vulnerable,
even so
I feel joy
because I feel you closer.
Thank you.

Carolyn Smyth

'Father, into your hands
I commit my spirit'

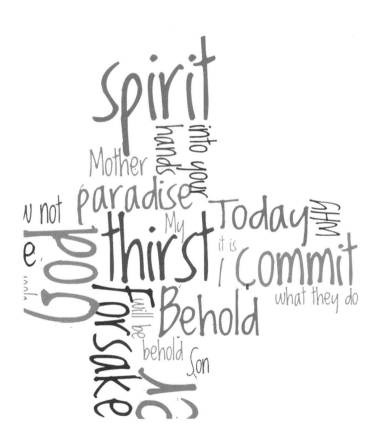

'Father, into your hands I commit my spirit.' (Luke 23:46, NIV)

He had been dying for a long time. Gasping for the air required to take the next breath. Death should have come before now. Yet still he fought on, unable or unwilling to give up. Unable or unwilling to acknowledge what lay ahead. For all the certainty of the outcome, Tom still hadn't spoken to his wife about it. For all the hours she had spent at his bedside, he refused to call them final hours, refused to accept she would soon be without him. After several months like this, and with the wisdom of many deaths behind him, the hospice doctor invoked the help of the spirit. He gently closed the door on the trinity of husband, wife and bottled whisky.

Time passed, the amber hourglass slowly drained and tumblers and words were exchanged in clumsy proxy for greater things. No one else on earth knows what was said that night, but she left late, tearful and unburdened. Tom left the next morning, finally giving up the suffocating coffin of his lungs.

It is no small matter to accept death. Even when it is inescapably close, like it was for Tom. Life is so precious, and so hard fought for that relinquishing it seems contrary to every basic urge, every higher function we possess. And yet here in Luke we see Christ accepting death. Staring it in the face and placing his spirit in the hands of God.

I met Tom during four months of hospice work as a medical student. Fourteen years later I have no idea what the names of most of the drugs were but I could tell you a lot about the people I met. It is a strange place to learn – people are dying and you are asking them questions they don't really need to answer. Yet time and again, folk would give some of their precious last moments to talk, to explain, to wonder at what it all meant.

Approaching these last words of Jesus feels very similar. This is holy ground, this dying business. Beyond the false piety of speaking in hushed tones a deeper reverence can emerge, even if we don't quite understand it. There are many mysteries here. I don't really know why Tom felt he couldn't let go, or how that was powerful enough to hold back death for many weeks. Nor can I explain the timing of finally talking about it and then dying the next morning. But explaining all of that is easy compared to explaining Christ's dying and his death. God in human form, God in crucified human form. We are deep in mystery now. Perhaps part of the problem is that this mystery is too familiar – we tame it so it doesn't cause too much upset. Church tradition says these are the very last words he said before death. Disturbing, provoking, unsettling in their very settledness, they cannot be dismissed lightly.

Jesus is dying – but we can join him for a while, sit with him and try to understand a little better. All questions seem inadequate to the task in hand, yet let's ask some anyway, in the hope they might help.

The question of intimacy

He speaks ancient words – reaching back beyond even 1st-century Palestine to the fifth verse of Psalm 31. As a devout Jew, Jesus would surely have been familiar with the whole psalm. It is a remarkable text to quote when dying (you may wish to go and read it now as an Easter meditation). What is most startling, however, is that it is not a direct quotation. Luke reports Jesus as saying 'Father', a word not found in Psalm 31. Thus there is a familiarity beyond the original context. Christ takes an intimate text and claims an additional level of intimacy.

Nestling either side of the phrase Christ quotes are further profound phrases: *'Free me from the trap that is set for me, for you are my refuge,'* and then *'redeem me, O Lord, the God of truth'.*

Neither makes any sense in light of a brutal execution. There was no freeing from the trap, no redemption. Not yet. They stand therefore as either a remarkable affirmation of faith at the bleakest point or a total and tragic religious delusion. Only time will tell.

The question of commitment

In an increasingly commodified culture, where the market has become a brutish god whose appetite must be satiated and yet never can be, some 'commodities' continue to defy quantification. Trust is one, and related to it is another, commitment. Politicians crave our trust, market brands plead for our commitment, religious salesmen peddle denuded copies – everyone wants us to commit, yet no one is willing to commit themselves.

Christ commits. It is a word that speaks of entrusting – as if this trust we cannot quantify can be carefully wrapped up and gifted to someone else. We stutter at this in our relationships, daily breaking the vows we make, fearful of loving yet desperately needing love. Christ commits.

Often when you are dying, words come at a cost. You choose them carefully and what you ask of others is laden with unspoken meaning. Especially concerning family members. Christ, in claiming God as his Father, then entrusts to God what is most precious. He entrusts his spirit – the essence of a person that comes from God in the first place (see how inadequate words are to the task here?).

To be fair, there was nothing left to give. In his life he had given everything – time, energy, wealth, devotion, learning, wisdom, compassion – all were poured out on behalf of others. To challenge, upset and drive out, heal, restore and forgive. A life in all its fulness. He gave it all and it was thrown back in his face in the shame of a criminal execution, abandoned by his 'followers', and forsaken by his God. Christ commits. He commits the only thing he has left to a Father who appears to have deserted him at the last. Yet still he commits.

The question of God-made-flesh

This intimacy, this commitment is an odd enough thing for anyone to express, but we inherit a claim that this man was actually God-made-flesh. This is no easy thing – least of all because here we have God-made-flesh entrusting his spirit into the 'hands' of God-not-made-flesh. Language breaks down again. Flesh is not spirit and spirit is not flesh. Though it is possible that such hard distinctions do not exist – that the line is fuzzier, God is both more physical and more spiritual than we can conceive.

And still there is more. Not just that God should take human form, not just that he should suffer and die, but that he accepts death without the certainty of resurrection, just as we must. It appears to me that Christ commits to his Father without a guaranteed outcome. Of course you can airbrush out this uncertainty, say of these words that Christ is giving himself back to God with his task complete. Sin atoned for, job done. But this appears to lessen the depth of suffering, abandonment and anguish that the cross must have been – surely more so for the God-man than it was for anybody else.

No, the cross must be darker than that if resurrection light is to shine out on the other side. Violence does not have the last word but it tries to. Violence wrought not by God but by humanity, trying to extinguish hope with wood, nails and a twisted and sick creativity. We do it all the time – we're very good at it. Just another execution in a forgotten corner of the Empire, as the system struggles to keep the peace. Let him say what he wants: he won't be here tomorrow:

'Father, into your hands I commit my spirit.'

Any faith that we express on our deathbeds seems pathetic without the strange and uncertain hope that there is more to come. We have no guarantee – and God knows what that feels like – but we do have an example of how accepting death is the way to defeat it, how trusting is possible at any point.

As Migliore says: *'To believe in the resurrection of Christ is to believe that God will not only triumph over the violent death that reigns in human history but also will triumph over the tragic death to which all life is presently subject.'*[1]
It is only belief, but it is remarkable stuff. Leading ever on to further mysteries and stranger questions. I do not pretend to understand it but somehow, through that death and raising back to life, Jesus is now committing his spirit into our hands. Soon, like Tom, we too must face death, but in the meantime, what will we do with Christ's spirit in our hands?

Loving God,
I fear death,
You embraced it.
I fear and crave intimacy in equal measure,
You make it possible.
I fear commitment,
You commit, again and again.

Christ, make my flesh your home,
my hands your hands.
My faltering love the starting point for your unwavering passion.
That my starving spirit might be renewed.
That the world might change, if only a little.

Even as I hesitate, hear me say:
Christ, into your hands I commit my spirit.

David McNeish

Note

1. Daniel Migliore, from Faith Seeking Understanding, *p.196, Eerdmans*

Beyond words

Beyond words

Jesus uttered a loud cry and breathed his last. (Mark 15:37, RSV)

Meditation

You were dying, Jesus.
You knew it.

The days of walking and preaching
and storytelling
were over.

You were struggling now to focus
struggling to breathe.

Friends, family, military, bystanders
they were all watching you

wondering if you had the strength for any more words
wondering if Elijah would come and save you
waiting for your end.

And you took a deep breath
and you cried out

and you died.

Your last sound, Jesus.

Your human life ending –
as it had begun in Bethlehem –
with a wordless cry.

A cry that was felt and understood by all present –
all friends
all strangers
all parents
all children
all creatures.

A cry that was felt and understood
and gathered up
in God.

Prayer

Jesus,
lover of life,
you died today.
You died as a hungry child
You died as a soldier in battle
You died in a flood
You died in a hospital bed
You died alone, away from home.

Jesus,
lover of life,
hear my crying
for those who die today
and for the pain that is in me and in the world.
Amen

Ruth Burgess

Good Friday prayer

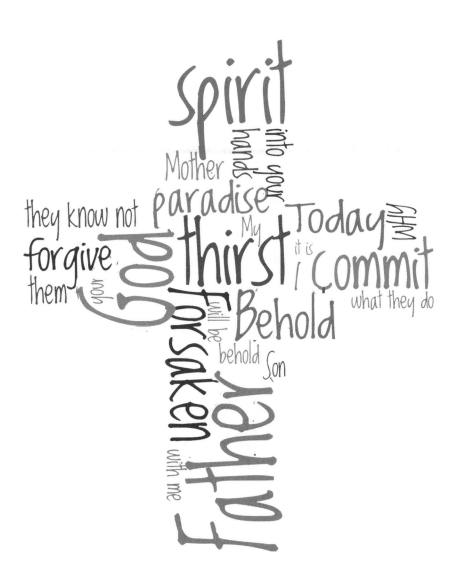

O Jesus, you weren't only crucified 2000 years ago.
You are being crucified today –
here and now ...

We pray for those who are being crucified here and now:

We pray for those being crucified by poverty:
in Sudan, in Easterhouse in Glasgow ...

For victims of capitalism and other Powers;
for those struggling under the burden of unfair debt and trade,
unfair debt and trade we profit by.

We pray for children being crucified.
Children working in sweatshops around the world.
Children who make the clothes we wear,
who help to harvest the food we eat.

We pray for women being crucified.
Women working in the sex trade in London, in Bangkok ...
Women who suffer abuse in our neighbourhoods
and in the neighbourhood of the world.
Women who suffer while we look away, deny, remain silent.

We pray for those being crucified by disease,
by AIDS, TB, malaria ...
Diseases which might be cured if only we'd choose life;
if only, as a nation, we didn't spend 30 billion pounds every year
on the military;
if only, as a world, we didn't spend over one trillion dollars U.S. a year
on death.

We pray for those being crucified in jails around the world,
in Saudi Arabia, Indonesia, Guatemala, Guantánamo Bay …
in countries and by countries whose governments
our government is happy to do business with
and to call close friends.

And we pray for this good earth,
this precious, fragile planet
we pay mock homage,
give poisoned streams to drink,
bind with fences,
strip and beat and flog,
pierce with spears until the blood and water pours out.

Jesus Christ,
we confess our complicity in all these crucifixions,
and in others.
Forgive us, Lord, we know not what we do.
Or do we?

We give thanks for individuals and organisations
working to bring healing and
hope in your world:

Church Action on Poverty
Oxfam
Save the Children
Christian Aid
Médecins Sans Frontières
Amnesty International

Earth First! ...

We give thanks for their passion and commitment.

Spirit of love,
help us to do all that we can to support them in their work;
help us to do more to ease suffering and to bring healing and hope,
in our neighbourhoods and in the neighbourhood of the world.

Christ has no other hands but our hands:
No other hands but our hands
to do God's work in the world.

Christ has no love but our love:
No love but our love to share with
the imprisoned, the silenced,
the persecuted, the marginalised ...

Amen

Neil Paynter

For Holy Saturday

The words from the Cross are traditionally part of the Good Friday liturgy. The short story which follows is a reflection for Holy Saturday. It reflects both the sorrow associated with Good Friday and the real hope of Easter Day …

Angel in Camden Town Market

I used to hear him busking in Camden Town Market.

He was a dwarf, or little person; his features sharp, and twisted from a diffi-
cult birth; beaten and scarred from a hard life. His arms were like broken
wings that had healed, and set crookedly. He played an autoharp, and sort
of strummed it with one hand and his long yellow nails. It sat in his lap. He
was perched on a high stool. There was a cap lying on the ground for
passers-by to throw change in.

The first time I heard him he was singing 'Summertime'. I was lost in the
maze of market stalls and myself, and was feeling cold and numb. His voice
made me stop … and shiver … as it opened me up.

His voice was a cry … In moments, soothing … victorious:

> *But one of these mornings …*
> *you're gonna rise up singing.*
> *You're gonna spread your wings*
> *and take to the skies …*
>
> *But until that morning …*
> *nothing's gonna harm you.*
>
> *So hush, little baby,*
> *don't you cry …*

It was a grey London day – cloudy, heavy, pressing, depressing. He looked
like an angel, perched on that stool: the autoharp was all silvery-sounding.
He sang 'Summertime' over and over. Like he was reciting a psalm. Like he

was praying for his broken self; and for every broken soul pushing and dragging themselves through Camden Town.

One time I stood and listened to him singing 'Summertime', and saw a flock of skylarks fly from out of his twisted mouth – bursting from the cage of his body, and trailing in a graceful arc up over scaffolding and steel and glass and rain-streaked concrete tombs …

I was working for a homeless shelter in King's Cross at the time. I went round London talking to people sleeping rough (my patch was Camden Town, the Strand, Kingsway, Temple, Piccadilly Circus …). I walked and rode around London so much that by the end of the day my snot was black with car exhaust and soot from the Underground.

But the real smell of London for me is the sweet fragrance of 'Old Holborne' rolling tobacco: its incense filled just about every conversation I had. I had a pouch of Old Holborne, and a packet of Rizla rolling papers, the shelter supplied me with. I'd offer folk I met a roll-up: 'Need a roll-up, mate?' It was a good 'opener' and a way in; we'd sit and talk. Later I'd ask them if they needed a kip for the night, and would invite them back to the shelter for a meal, a break from the wind and cold, some hours of unguarded sleep …

I had the angel's voice singing in my head all through one day doing street work …

… Talking to a young guy on the Strand, who'd just got out of prison. In prison he'd spent all his free time using the weights and exercise equipment in the yard, he tells me. At first, it was a way to stay sane and out of trouble, but then he got into it – and now his idea is to do a moduled course at college he heard about, and then get a job in a health club: showing other people how to use the machines, and helping them to get healthy and fit.

He can do it, he tells me, with sinew in his voice – and I believe him ... He can *do* anything, *survive* anything, he says. One time he almost died from drugs and drink. He OD'd and passed out: he remembers the blackness. 'Like a pit.' ... They rushed him to hospital and gave him a shot of adrenaline in his heart ... He feels *himself* when he's working out, he says to me.

I offer him a roll-up but he says he doesn't smoke. 'Oh, of course,' I say ... I offer him a kip back at the shelter but he tells me he's moving on tonight. Whenever he feels like he's getting sucked into a pit now, he moves on. He rolls up his jacket, and shows me his arm, tattooed with a bald eagle – it's like solid rock.

> *... you're gonna spread your wings,*
> *and take to the skies ...*

Talking to another young guy, skippering outside Burger King; who, after his silent, hard friends all leave, admits to me that he's scared ... Scared of going to court and being sent back to jail. 'Scared of going down the cages and getting slashed' ...

He wants his mum, he says, sucking on a bottle of beer. And I want to hug him.

> *... So hush, little baby,*
> *don't you cry ...*

Talking to old Harry. Sitting cross-legged on the cold stone floor of King's Cross station, sharing a big bottle of cider as he recites to me his poem about the American West. About Geronimo and Sitting Bull, and how the U.S. government betrayed the Native American people and stole their land.

Harry was a miner; his family had worked the land for generations: 'Until Thatcher came ridin' into town and gave the country to the corporations and bankers.'

After that – after the marches and the battles with police on horseback, and then the years of never being able to find any real work – he 'lost heart' and 'something deep down inside of him died'. He calls himself a drunk, a failure: he ran out on his family.

But his heart's alive when he recites his beautiful, human poetry. He waves his arms like a prophet, like a shaman. And everyone just walks past the dirty old drunk – radiating light; intoxicated with the Spirit … And as the Transport Police cowboys come to arrest him to dump him in a cell overnight, he is as stoic as Sitting Bull; his face deeply life-lined as Geronimo's in the American neon light.

> *… But until that morning*
> *nothing's gonna harm you …*

Talking to young Robbie on the steps of St Pancras Church. About the Beatles, and their song from *Revolver* 'Tomorrow Never Knows': *'Play the game ex-is-tence to the end … of the beginning,'* he intones, and laughs hollowly, and stares at me with his wide, dead eyes. Like black holes. He drones that he's looking forward to dying and becoming atoms … to being infinite and for ever. And I'm not sure what to answer. I get sucked up into his eyes for a moment. I see oblivion, I see Hell … There are no stars in young Robert's eyes any more; and I turn away as he finishes shooting up.

> *… One of these mornings …*
> *you're gonna spread your wings*
> *and take to the skies …*

Talking to Chas up near Westminster Station – who runs up and tells me that he made the Homelessness World Cup football team! He went for a try-out – and made the team! And now he's going on an aeroplane to Brazil to play for his country!

> *... you're gonna spread your wings*
> *and take to the skies ...*

Talking to a guy whose girlfriend and best friend were killed together in a car crash, and who's got a lot of pills on him, and keeps popping them while we're talking, washing them down with a bottle of vodka he keeps slugging back. He hands over the bottle of pills at one point, but then takes them back again when I fumble around nervously and say something stupid, when I lose hold on the conversation and it seems like I'm not *really* listening and don't *really* care. I think of snatching the bottle back, but everything's happening so fast; and as I'm just about to, he lurches off into the Underground. I push my way through a crowd, but by the time I get inside the station he's far away. And as I watch him riding deep down on the conveyor belt of death, and disappear, I say a short prayer:

> *But until that morning ...*
> *nothing's gonna harm you ...*

Talking to a tired, faded-looking woman who tells me her name is Rose; who escaped her husband: who was over 20 stone, and made her cook and clean up after him. Who made her wipe his arse while he called her mother.

She's got nowhere to go now – nowhere to go but she's free, she says, and tilts her face up to the pale London sun; and there's a trail of perfume of something like roses from a smartly-dressed woman who passes, on her way to the theatre.

… Nothing's gonna harm you …

Talking to an old guy kipping in a little park, who's dying for a smoke; who plays the harmonica, and tells me that it's nice to play in the early morning with the birds singing … I sit with him on the bench, and he talks to me about dancing with his wife. 40 years ago at a dancehall in London. He wore a zoot suit; she wore a long flowing ballgown that shimmered with light when she moved … He tells me that he'll see her again in heaven, and that they'll dance again together there; and sits and smokes, and quietly plays his harp.

But one of these mornings
you're gonna rise up singing …

So hush, little baby,
don't you cry …

Talking to the Rastafarian who feeds the birds, who has feathers and twigs matted in his long, cabled hair; who tells me that the songbirds can communicate with the angels. And also with the free and funky-great spirit of William Blake, who lives in Soho Square.

Talking to Marcus, who's waiting to get the keys for his new place: He started a new job as a bricklayer, and took his first pay and put it down on a room. Before, he was a miner, a labourer … He won't get in until the first of the month, but that's OK, he says – he's got a job. Meanwhile, he keeps to himself; keeps himself tidy, keeps away from the drink. 'Sometimes you just gotta wait,' he says, and sits and waits. Listens to football on his transistor radio …

He says that when he moves into his flat, the first thing he'll do is to make himself a nice big meal – a nice fry-up: eggs, sausages, beans, tomatoes, mushrooms – he's got a television a friend's keeping for him – and sit and watch football and eat his fry-up. He's *really* looking forward to that, he tells me.

> *… But until that morning …*
> *nothing's gonna harm you …*

Talking to Kostas from Greece, who carries a terrible weight of papers around with him everywhere in an old backpack. Papers that prove who is: where he was born; where he's lived – in a hostel in Germany, in a refugee camp in France; where he's worked – picking fruit in Spain, hops in Kent, cleaning toilets in an old-age home …

'My dream is that – one day – I will carry on me only a phone, a wallet, and keys,' he says, and sets his burden down a minute to rest and have a roll-up. I give him a light and he sighs out smoke; closes his baggy eyes a moment … Then takes a deep breath, and picks up his heavy backpack again. I watch him walk off down Euston Road, bowed like Atlas.

… one day …
You're gonna spread your wings and
take to the skies …

Talking to Mary, who was knackered; and who winced and cried and went through bloody hell with her swollen legs and infected foot to get to the night shelter with me – on the bus, on the tube, on the tube, on the bus –

getting dragged up and down the fucking stairs and escalators … And who, by the end of the night, was somehow singing and dancing to country-and-western music in the shelter common room.

But one of these mornings …
you're gonna rise up singing.
You're gonna spread your wings and
take to the skies …

But until that morning …
nothing's gonna harm you.
So hush, little baby,
don't you cry …

Neil Paynter

'Summertime', by George and Ira Gershwin, from the opera Porgy and Bess. *(One of the most emotive and beautiful versions of 'Summertime' was recorded by Janis Joplin, not long before her death in 1970.)*

www.simoncommunity.org.uk

spirit

Mother

into your hands

paradise

they know not

My

Today

AHM

forgive

thirst

it is

i commit

what they do

them

your

God

Behold

I will be

Forsaken

behold

Son

Father

with me

About the authors

Ruth Burgess is a member of the Iona Community and is retired. Her books include *Eggs and Ashes: Practical and Liturgical Resources for Lent and Holy Week* (with Chris Polhill) and *Fire and Bread: Resources for Easter Day to Trinity Sunday* (Wild Goose Publications).

Donald Eadie is a Methodist minister who had to retire early due to a serious spinal condition which has required three major operations. He lives much of his life in a loved room to which people come not for therapy or counselling but as those who also seek the life-giving presence of God within this wondrous and terrifying world, and within the story of our lives. Donald is discovering that 'the borderlands' are the context where God's Spirit works to convert the Church. He is the author of *Grain in Winter: Reflections for Saturday People* (Epworth Press).

David McNeish worked as a hospital doctor, worship musician and campaigner for the CAB service before admitting defeat and training as a Church of Scotland minister. He lives in South Queensferry with his wife, Sally, and three young children. He is a member of the Iona Community.

Peter Millar is a well-known writer and campaigner for justice and peace and a former Warden of Iona Abbey who spent many years in India. He is also closely involved with the work of the Wellspring Community in Australia. He is based in Edinburgh. His books include *Waymarks: Signposts to Discovering God's Presence in the World* (Canterbury Press), and *Our Hearts Still Sing: Daily Readings* (Wild Goose Publications).

Neil Paynter is the editor of a number of books, Editor of *Coracle*: the magazine of the Iona Community, and author of *Down to Earth: Stories and*

Sketches (Wild Goose Publications). Previously, he worked in the social service field, in homeless shelters, in nursing homes for the elderly and in rest homes for individuals with mental health challenges.

Jan Sutch Pickard is a poet and storyteller living on the Isle of Mull. Collections of poems include *Out of Iona: Words from a Crossroads of the World* and *Between High and Low Water: Sojourner Songs* (Wild Goose Publications). A former Warden of Iona Abbey, Jan has recently served in the West Bank with the Ecumenical Accompaniment Programme in Palestine and Israel. As well as travelling round bearing witness to that situation, she spends a lot of time – when not collecting driftwood for her fire and seaweed for her potato beds – preparing and leading worship, mostly on Mull and Iona. She is a member of the Iona Community.

David Rhodes is a writer on spirituality and social justice. His work with homeless people led to Retreats on the Streets (www.cuf.org.uk/pray/retreat-street), currently forming the core of the Church Urban Fund's 2011 Lent course. His books include *Sparrow Story*, a gritty retelling of the Gospel set in present-day Palestine, and *Faith in Dark Places* (www.turbulentbooks.co.uk). He is an associate member of the Iona Community.

Carolyn Smyth is a member of the Iona Community, a minister of the United Reformed Church, a worship enabler, a prison befriender and aspires to being a graffiti artist.

Alison Swinfen is a member of the Iona Community; author of *Through Wood: Prayers and Poems Reconnecting with the Forest* (Wild Goose Publications); Co-Convener of Glasgow Refugee, Asylum and Migration Network; Professor of Languages and Intercultural Studies at the University of Glasgow; and Advisor to the World Council of Churches International Ecumenical Peace Convocation working group.

Also from Wild Goose Publications:

Lent & Easter Readings from Iona
Neil Paynter
Lent offers an opportunity to see the world afresh. This book of readings from members and staff of the Iona Community aims to help us reappraise our lives during the period leading up to Easter.
ISBN 9781901557626

Eggs and Ashes
Ruth Burgess & Chris Polhill
Modern, relevant resources to accompany readers through Lent and Easter for many years, with material for Shrove Tuesday, Ash Wednesday, Mothering Sunday, Palm Sunday and Holy Week, as well as suggestions for a Lent discipline.
ISBN 9781901557879

Fire and Bread
Ruth Burgess
Prayers, responses, liturgies, songs, poems, reflections, meditations, sermons and stories, covering the weeks from Easter Day to Trinity Sunday, including Ascension Day, Pentecost, Saints' days, Rogation days, environmental days and many more.
9781905010301

www.ionabooks.com

Iona Dawn
Neil Paynter
The dramatic events of the days leading up to Easter Sunday expressed through biblical readings and reflections provide an insightful guide to Holy Week.
ISBN 9781905010110

Stages on the Way
The Wild Goose Worship Group
Traces Jesus' road to the cross through Lent, Holy Week and Easter. Its prime purpose is to resource worship that enables people to sense the hope, apprehension and joy of Easter as felt by Jesus' friends. The range and diversity offers a unique source of elements for lay and clergy worship planners and enablers.
ISBN 9781901557114

Enemy of Apathy
John L Bell/Graham Maule
Songbook containing 62 songs and chants for Lent, Eastertide and Pentecost. Includes: Travelling the road to freedom * Be still and know * Jesus Christ is waiting * Lord of the morning * Kyrie/Sanctus & Benedictus/Agnus Dei (Kentigern setting) etc.
ISBN 9780947988272

Wild Goose Publications is part of the Iona Community, which is:

- An ecumenical movement of men and women from different walks of life and different traditions in the Christian church
- Committed to the gospel of Jesus Christ, and to following where that leads, even into the unknown
- Engaged together, and with people of goodwill across the world, in acting, reflecting and praying for justice, peace and the integrity of creation
- Convinced that the inclusive community we seek must be embodied in the community we practise

Together with our staff, we are responsible for:

- Our islands residential centres of Iona Abbey, the MacLeod Centre on Iona, and Camas Adventure Centre on the Ross of Mull

and in Glasgow:

- The administration of the Community
- Our work with young people
- Our publishing house, Wild Goose Publications
- Our association in the revitalising of worship with the Wild Goose Resource Group

The Iona Community was founded in Glasgow in 1938 by George MacLeod, minister, visionary and prophetic witness for peace, in the context of the poverty and despair of the Depression. Its original task of rebuilding the monastic ruins of Iona Abbey became a sign of hopeful rebuilding of community in Scotland and beyond. Today, we are about 250 Members, mostly in Britain, and 1500 Associate Members, with 1400 Friends worldwide. Together and apart, 'we follow the light we have, and pray for more light'.

For information on the Iona Community contact:
The Iona Community, Fourth Floor, Savoy House, 140 Sauchiehall
Street, Glasgow G2 3DH, UK. Phone: 0141 332 6343
e-mail: admin@iona.org.uk; web: www.iona.org.uk

For enquiries about visiting Iona, please contact:
Iona Abbey, Isle of Iona, Argyll PA76 6SN, UK. Phone: 01681 700404
e-mail: ionacomm@iona.org.uk